All Will Fall Away

poems by

Karen S. Henry

Finishing Line Press
Georgetown, Kentucky

All Will Fall Away

For my husband, Tom—my love, my life

Copyright © 2020 by Karen S. Henry
ISBN 978-1-64662-367-9 First Edition
All rights reserved under International and Pan-American Copyright Conventions. No part of this book may be reproduced in any manner whatsoever without written permission from the publisher, except in the case of brief quotations embodied in critical articles and reviews.

ACKNOWLEDGMENTS

Thanks to the editors of the publications where the following poems first appeared:

BoomerLitMag.com, "Galveston Blues" and "The Lost Whaling Museum"
Crosswinds, "Taste"
Stoneboat, "Birch Bark"
Zoetic Press: *The Literary Whip* podcast, *Persephone Suite*

Publisher: Leah Huete de Maines
Editor: Christen Kincaid
Cover Art: Karen S. Henry
Author Photo: Thomas C. Henry
Cover Design: Elizabeth Maines McCleavy

Order online: www.finishinglinepress.com
also available on amazon.com

Author inquiries and mail orders:
Finishing Line Press
P. O. Box 1626
Georgetown, Kentucky 40324
U. S. A.

Table of Contents

Taste 1

Galveston Blues 2

The Burn 4

Birch Bark 5

Flower Dream 6

Sleepless 7

Feeling the Excitement of Being in Love 8

Five Dreamers in This House of Dreams 9

Overlay 10

Frost Fire 11

The Work of the Forest 12

The Lost Whaling Museum 13

Spell to Retrieve a Lost One 15

Taking in the Docks 17

You Drift 19

Her Garden in Winter 21

Figures on the Edge 22

At Home in America 26

Persephone Suite

    Persephone's Report 28

    Hades' Complaint 29

    Zeus' Answer 30

    Pomegranate Seeds 31

    A Hummingbird in Hell 34

Taste

Taste what no one said would be good for you
the sharp burn of that shot on Bourbon Street
poured down your throat by the angeldevil
who tried to sell you more.

Taste the loneliness of that solo horn
across the street—
he has no shoes
only the ache in his song
that plays behind your eyes.

Your own songs spill out
like streams threading a silver path
through stones
but they run dry
and you've come to the city of floods.

Taste what is put in front of you
sharp and salty and bitter, it urges you on
the throbbing lights of a city
unhinged by pleasure
seeking and sickness
by the din of fear
of waters rising.

Taste the chicory and the gumbo
the sweet meat of the bottom feeders
the crawfish scrabbling in the silt
the greens and the sticky remains.

Taste the stirrings of an urge
to be gone from all you know
to follow the river to that delta
to let it all spill out.

Galveston Blues

Pacing the hard sand of Galveston
two miles to the eastern tip
you thought a sprawling shrimper
was a broken airplane
sinking in the fog-bound distance.
You called the Coast Guard
who were too polite to doubt your SOS
out loud.
Maybe they did send a boat.
We probably ate the guy's catch
later that night in the Juju
listening to the blues.
This island knows how to sing them.
Wanting to wail and cry
in Mardi Gras drag
with the keen guitar.
Lost souls,
like the 6,000 swept away in the storm
that shattered the island to splinters
on the brink of their glory.
Time seeped away from them then,
—the surge that battered them all night
left them dry and wrung out before dawn.

No two singers sing the same blues.
They sing the same words
even the same tune.
They dig over and over
with the same phrase
but cut through to different pain.

When we left Galveston for the mainland
we heard those Mardi Gras blues
singing the tankers and the rigs
and the cruise ships
lighting out for the glittering south
and the voices left behind

on the sea wall
staring into the fog's mouth
singing one blue note
over and over.

The Burn

Let's spare the moss huts
and mushrooms
while we burn the forest around them.
Old pine boughs moldering
for years
under the snow-felled trees
of late March.
You would burn it all
if you could
one great conflagration,
clear the woods
of scrub pine, wild cherry, sassafras,
turn it all to meadow
rolling under the sputter
of woodpeckers at the edge.

When you stare
into the orange heart of fire
sinking into gray ash
do you remember
the burns when we were young
and our children shrieked
at the burst of embers
flying high?

Your arms—once undefeated
hang heavy
yet you stay to the end
turning the ashes
over and over.

The black-capped chickadees
sing on—their plaintive cry
lighting the woods that remain
with their own kind of fire.

Birch Bark

A message from the birch
furled at my door—
I cannot read
handwriting so thin
it blends in with the veins.
I am content to let it rest unread,
I, who once tried to discern
the secrets of the universe.

Gold finches
crack seeds above yellow lilies.
A gold bug glittering in the grass
catches my eye
but it spreads gilded wings
and disappears.

My gold wedding band
with its silver center
now scratched by years of use
still anchors me.

We follow separate paths
more often than before
laughing over the memory
of early times
when I would cry
at the separation
of sleep.

We share dreams
and children, now grown.
Their lives unwinding
like our own
to ends we cannot see.

The birch grows beyond our reach,
its silver messages ever peeling
and falling softly on the grass
still green.

Flower Dream

Spring flowers everywhere
in the house
and outside
in neoclassical glass urns
and metal pots on the roof.
You displayed them
big flowering branches
of rhododendron and azalea
mounds of pink and white flowers
—in your pruning
you wasted nothing.
Everywhere I looked
immense vases
filled with effervescent water
like champagne
bubble trails surging to the top.

This was your gift
in the dream—and why not?
Like Bacchus, with you
everything flows.

Sleepless

A long night of half dreams
flashes of light
commands to climb down the ladder of sleep
unheeded.
Your breathing troubled me.
The faint O of a cry
drove you far away.
We took turns going under
then lapping the shore of waking.

In the end
I was your guardian.
I felt you running
in the fresh green grass
beside me.

Feeling the Excitement of Being in Love

In a long white dress
wearing my lover's shoes
through the mud
arm in arm with this dark-haired man
I had to tell him
we were in this together
moving swiftly to the bath house
feeling the excitement
of being in love.

Five Dreamers in This House of Dreams

The old mother who dreams her back
        is straight again.

Her son, in a death grip
        with his brother
looking serene this night
        as if their fight is over.

His daughter, who ran all day
her feet shuffling still
        under the covers.

Her brother
dreaming of love
        lost and found
and of a song he can barely hear
he knows he should be singing.

Their mother, left to herself,
who keeps meeting old friends
        shifting places
drifting in from every corner
of her vanishing days.

Overlay

The October cries of insects
still rhythmic but slow
with an occasional pulse
      of curiosity
           in the overlay
as if love could have another chance
this late in the season.

Frost Fire

Last week mist rose from the marsh.
This morning gorse is dipped in frost
like sparklers with their hard coats
ready to burst into stars
if the sun hits them.

It's the season of waiting
the season of silence.
Clouds cast us into a gray solitude
most days.

But when the rare sun
lights up the trees
and each bright berry
is a circle of fire
signaling plenty to the birds,
we rejoice.

The Work of the Forest

The work of the forest is slow.
Mushrooms grow
on downed trees
for many seasons.
Rough red caps push
through pine needles,
white quarters spin
on delicate stems,
strong shelves make a ladder
up a dead tree
still standing,
charred ghost pipe remains,
under chicken of the woods.
But the curious probe
with thin rods
far below
to check the warming earth
for fever.
Do mushroom teeth
set on edge
by rising heat
nibble quicker to the core
of logs crumbling to dust
in record time?
Can cooling breezes
reverse the trend?
Will rain return
to douse the western fires?
Perhaps we all need a berth
on Elon's spaceship
to see the earth—
that blue bubble
in a black sea
ready to pop.

The Lost Whaling Museum

The jawbones of whales
should be buried here.
They hung from the ceiling
of the old whaling museum
weeks ago, it seems,
but it's decades.

With all the loot from the Kendall,
they were shipped off to New Bedford
like countless whalers before them
centuries ago.

Now peace reigns
over the green lawns
of the Kendall.
The stone mermaid
under her gray bench
watches pensively
over the field she defended
where priapic mushrooms
once spread.
Now ravaged,
they were scraped clean
by Puritan blades
at Thanksgiving
—the mystery
of their riotous uprising
lost forever.

I live here.
Once I pored over the journals
of old whaling captains,
gazed at the wooden mastheads
carved to resemble
wives and daughters
left behind.

I tread these woods
under a Renoir sky
in December
wondering what artifacts of ours
will remain
tools of our trade
memory chips and wands
pixels logging voyages
through dreams
or nightmares.

Where will those who come after us
send our remains?
To some bustling star
or to a cave deep in the earth
they left behind?

Spell to Retrieve a Lost One

We've said the prayers
to make you come around.
You're far too gone for those.
You lost your way
at the back of the woods
where all the thickets close.
No one who remembers
can enter.
I see the paths of your mind
disappearing
like a fast-forward nature show
where the tangled growth returns
over asphalt in an instant.

You are lost
but forging on
stumbling while
harried on all sides.
Fearful of cliffs
where there are only lines in linoleum,
you cannot take in
the angels at your side.
Their presence
terrifies
until they come around
to face you
and say your name.

Still you are alone.
You know no one.
You're irretrievable
but we conjure you—
the memory of you
who have no memory
the bright image
of your strength and surety
before the dark claimed you.

May you go safely
through the trackless woods
and cross that dream bridge
spanning marsh
where those lost forever without names
murmur your name.

Taking in the Docks
    (From Suite for Jeanne)

Under gray clouds
like dim pearls
with water light spilling over
they wear rubber clothes
and gaiters
in the cold mud.

Last weekend they were at play
with cases of beer
and sun squinting
across the lake,
a take-down party
with no serious aim.

But today
in the dull gray afternoon
they've backed the truck
down to the dirty shore
and two by two
they haul up all the planks
and stack them
on the shallow bed
until the truck is full
and pulls away.

I'm in my red kayak
just twice my height
bouncing against
the stiffening wind
water slurping over the bow
with each wave
I hit head on
the wind drawing me to the center
though I am bent shoreward
the cold stealing through me.

This operation of taking everything in
that meant life and freedom
until a new season of warmth
and bright water
hurts me.
I give in to the cold gray
and pull my small craft
onto the sand.

There she is
with her porous face
and bandages.
They're shutting off
the fatal medicine
and letting her go,
a small boat
floating free on the
enormous sea.
She has to pick her path
without a paddle—
that's checked for the season—
all her effort
bent to steering
no chance of putting in to shore
the docks are gone.

You Drift
    (From Suite for Jeanne)

You drift now
after strife.
They said you slept
but I knew you heard.
I dreamt I held your hand
and sang shape songs
"What wondrous love is this
  to send such perfect peace?"
but that wasn't your kind of music.

Doo-wop sings us
into your absence
"The Chapel of Love."
Then the song from your partner
"They Can't Take That Away from Me."
He cherished what remained
each time something new
was burned away.

When I asked
if you could get back
to that gracious woman
who said thanks to everyone
you laughed
and said it was the drugs.

I feared that we would
have to wrest the fight
from your hands.
That dark angel on your shoulder
demon-charging your breath
with steady fury.

Instead, you drifted
into that ocean
where all life empties,

like a child
who relinquishes
the finger she grasped
so tightly.
Sleep just came
and released her grip
her fear
her want

leaving her to drift
into dreams
that resolve
what they resolve
what maybe
love alone
resolves.

Her Garden in Winter

Her breath moves like mist
on wisteria sheathed in ice.
In winter light
her hands and face
are fields of shadow.

There beside the Japanese yew
she bends,
her small hard palms
work the dirt
and underneath
the cramped roots breathe.

Knees ache on the frozen sod,
fingers, too stiff to bend,
knock a stone against the ice
to free
one more seedling.

Scrub from the hill
takes root in her lawn
growing to evergreen
crowned with cones.

She stands between
wild brush and a garden,
between two natures:
she's rooted in a green life
giving over to the cold.

Figures on the Edge

1.

Before first light
she wakes to cook the beans
to knead cornmeal
to press tortillas
her lot, the one to stay
to watch, to guard, to wait
daughter, sister, aunt,
not mother.

Her sisters, the ones to travel
far from their children
to lands richer than their own
Belize, Costa Rica, Spain.
They yearn at night
for their children
and dream of Elda.

I am the visitor she feeds.
Her English matches my Spanish.
We talk in present tense
even about the past.
Family photos dot the walls
of the small house.
She points to herself
in a graduation gown
a shy smile of success.

She is the one to stay
to fetch water and wood
to feed the chickens
dry the tears
of the boy and girl
who miss their mothers.

The one to stand beside her father
cowboy hat and a mouthful of stars.
His sister tends her grandson
fourteen but stricken
who lies across her lap
and moans, Rosa, a pietà
with a living boy.

And Elda who teaches me
Spanish words,
and how to eat alone at a table
while each one watches
and waits for a turn
to use the single plate and cup.

Elda, whose fierce life
burns within her
at a steady temperature
who wakes each day
to take up the appointed tasks
with no visible sign
of desire unrequited.

2.

He is only six.
He curses his teacher
calling her a bitch
who strips for money.

He wants to blow the horns at every turn
knock down any wall—just watch him.

He hoists my laptop overhead
eyes wide
mouth stretched.

I imagine it crashing to the floor
all those words spilling out
to nowhere.

She holds him down gently
calls for backup
one at his shoulders
one at his knees
"How are we safe?"
she asks
over and over
till he lies still.

Joshua, only six.
How will you make your way
in the world
on the edge of oblivion?
Your mother crying
in the office
for mercy.
How will you learn?

In this class of the unshackled
where any word lights a fuse
only supple wills can douse.
I fear for you, my dear
destroyer—
my little man who adores
violation.

3.

She makes her way
gripping the bag of peels and shells.
I watch her meager progress
turn the frozen yard

into a vast tundra.
Her bent shape
skims the dull horizon
like one of the Norns
bearing the dying world
on her back,
the fates of all
in her thin hand
holding still.
Entering her tenth decade
the end ever in sight now
she wonders what the day can bring
that she has never seen.

These three meet in me
on the darkest night
waiting for the turn
into light.

At Home in America

I'm trying to remember
the country where I felt
in the end
most people are good.
I remember the hills
and mountains I've climbed.

Oaks and maples on Moose Hill
the keen scent of pine needles
under late summer sun
and ferns along the trails—
ghosts of revolutionary soldiers
and first people.

Snows in June on Mount Rainier
dripping eucalyptus
and redwoods
moss so thick
I could bed down on it.

Bear grass and ptarmigan
in Glacier where I hiked as a girl
and biked decades later
on the Highway to the Sun
a native trail.

As a child I climbed on the steely cannons
of Valley Forge
and ran on the stippled grass
over countless dead
not knowing.

Grew up
trying to rise
through dark water
to consciousness.

Millions on the move
fleeing homes
that implode
with impossible choices.
Every day the violent grin
in the doorway
as children grow
more timid.

I heard about a child
who was finally returned
to his mother
—just five years old.
Now, he hides when strangers enter;
his favorite game
patting down
and shackling migrants.

Persephone Suite

Persephone's Report

For days before
I had sad dreams
of lost friends
betraying me.

That day I went out to win.
One flower led to another
fragrance of narcissus
led me on.

I turned to face
the cold shadow
looming over me.
There was no sudden grab.
Joy froze in me
then seeped out
in the dark.

Of course I ate the seeds.
What else was there to do
in that empty space
exhausting beyond words?

Hades' Complaint

It's all chance.
I love the light
but my lot was the underworld.
I hone the point of my chariot
to rip through stone
dividing day from night.
I took what I saw.
When she was mine,
she took my bribe.
"What's left for you?"

She loses color in the dark
and motion
becoming so still
with eyes half open
she looks like one of us.

So, she's not happy here.
I'm happy when I see her.
Even the dead have to live.

Zeus' Answer

The high blue dome
and long shadows
tilt toward autumn.

Time to move again
leaving a wake
of black basil.

Heavy scent
settles around her—
she's already gone.

White smoke curls up
out of the crater,
feeble thanks from my brother.

Frozen sleet,
the curse of my erstwhile lover
who never forgives.

What was I to do?
Laws fix the world.
I bent—could not break them.

Girls fall into pools.
She's lucky she wasn't changed
into a spring of endless tears.

Pomegranate Seeds

(Demeter)

When
my girl first
went under, I froze
rivers seeking her wan face. Where
was my joking darling, my 3-D checker mate?
Gatorade labels scratched off
and scattered like petals
a poor sign of
unforeseen
despair.

Where
she landed
after her abduction by
unremitting sadness is beyond
me—Hades never took me anywhere.
But my rage at her lacerations
her brutal suffocation
raised the stony god
who gave us only
half life.

How
she survived
in that world of shadows
mystifies me still—makes me fear
she'll go under again to eat more seeds.
He gave her six months for life
no possibility of parole.
I stole the harvest
starved men
gave in.

(Persephone)

Why
didn't you find
me before I lost myself?
Lost from birth, I suppose, I
could only lose myself further.
Still, you owe me a whole life
someone does, someone
I can't find no matter
how hard I
seek.

(Hades)

How you mistake me.
I want simply to save
our sweet girl. Here
in this rich dark all
her dreams are real.

(Zeus)

I
am
the one
who made you
who loved you first
who left you on your own.
I have the whole earth to cherish.
Do you think I can cut you cosmic slack?
Even I couldn't hold all the pieces in place if I did.
I release you to your fate, to your love, to your hate.

(Demeter)

Why
go through
this harsh world
when in the end all
will fall away to ash?
I step in the meadow
the fragrant air sings
through me
I am
here.

A Hummingbird in Hell

The whir and halt and tilt and swoop
to shoot across the green
to a new world of tubular blooms
takes all of me

but a small piece of pain.

I'm a creature in the sun
half my days.
The dark ice of death
doesn't own me yet.

Why can't I flit and stoop
hover and sip blooms while I may?
Yes, there's the devil to pay.
Yes, I'm growing old in the dank underworld.
Yes, I cannot love my overlord.
Yes, I pity myself endlessly.
Yes, I am bored.
Yes, I miss my sunlit summer—
the long hours of azure and heat.
What of that?

I'm rising, turning, spinning, diving
in a thrill even here, even now—
the scent of salvia spurs me on
beyond the burst of strength
in my wings
beyond necessity
beyond even the thirst
to know why
I am here.

Karen S. Henry collaborated with director Herbert Blau and the experimental theater company KRAKEN, of which she was a member, in writing and performing *Elsinore*, based on *Hamlet*, and *Crooked Eclipses: A Theatrical Essay on Shakespeare's Sonnets*. With her husband, Thomas Henry, she co-founded the Boston Theater Group, whose major works (supported by the National Endowment for the Arts, the Massachusetts Arts Council, and the New England Foundation for the Arts), include *The Burrow*, based on Kafka's story; *Metamorphoses*, a reflection on Ovid's great work; *The Beloved: The Story of Ruth*; and *The Long Light: Voices of Aging*, a piece combining a wide variety of poetry from Whitman and Dickinson to Atwood and Levertov, along with monologues written by Henry and Alison Luterman. *The Long Light* toured throughout Massachusetts to schools, churches, and senior citizen centers and served as a catalyst for discussions about aging and memory. The group also created a version of *Crooked Eclipses*, which premiered in Boston, and a brief version of this piece that toured to schools and colleges in Massachusetts.

In addition to these theater pieces, the Boston Theater Group produced two operas with composer W. Newell Hendricks: *The Cell*, based on a play about political action written by Henry; and *Ascona*, about counter-cultural figures in the early twentieth century, including Frieda and D. H. Lawrence, expressionist dancer Mary Wigman, early environmental poet and activist Gusto Graser, and radical psychoanalyst Otto Gross. For these operas, Hendricks and Henry received two National Endowment composer/librettist fellowships.

Henry currently works with Row Twelve Contemporary Music Ensemble as performer and writer, creating dozens of poetry/music pieces and collaborating with other poets, musicians, and dancers. Her poems have recently appeared in *BoomerLit Mag, Crosswinds Poetry Journal, The Literary Whip* podcast of *Zoetic Press, and Stoneboat Literary Journal*.

After a long career in publishing with Bedford/St. Martin's of Macmillan, Henry now works with Innovations for Learning, a nonprofit organization that creates literacy software for elementary school students in urban districts across the country and recruits corporate volunteers to work with these students to help them learn to read. She earned a B.A. from Oberlin College and a Ph.D. from Tufts University, with a dissertation on the mirror in Shakespeare. She lives in Sharon, Massachusetts, with her husband Tom, and her mother-in-law, Ruth, and she enjoys frequent visits from her grown children, Daniel and Juliana.

www.ingramcontent.com/pod-product-compliance
Lightning Source LLC
LaVergne TN
LVHW041551070426
835507LV00011B/1043